Praise for *In This Distance*

Brooke Sahni pulls off the damn near impossible with this book: elegant, precise, and piercingly aware poems about love and the erotic. A lot of poets treat these subjects as kryptonite. Those who tackle them usually fall into traps. Not here. Sahni's brilliant exploration is unflinching and unearths a goldmine of wisdom, one as luminous as it is enthralling.

—HAYAN CHARARA, author of *These Trees, Those Leaves, This Flower, That Fruit*

Brooke Sahni's In This Distance gathers the great branches of existence—love, family, connection; hunger, spirit, ritual; risk, betrayal, loss—into the pyre of sensuality. It's a stirring collection of odes (and O!) to Esther Perel and Audre Lorde, two of our culture's foremost goddess-scholars of desire, alongside 21st century love poems: Sahni's work is intimate, pansexual, feminist, self-aware, fragmented, orgasmic. In This Distance is a carnal prayer book full of lines as beautifully wrought as bobbin lace, lines of 'sacred tenderness' and the blinding light of a woman surrendering to her own vast erotic power.

—ARIELLE GREENBERG, author of *I Live in the Country & Other Dirty Poems*

Praise for *Brooke Sahni*

Fearlessly mixing the divine and spiritual with the secular and mundane, Sahni challenges the very definitions of holiness and devotion.

—CLEVELAND REVIEW OF BOOKS

Layers of sacred teaching, Jewish and Sikh, inform these youthful reflections on language and identity . . . Childhood memories fall together with mourning for relatives who take their precious old-world knowledge with them; desire to adhere to ancient traditions vie with moments of sensual adolescent self-discovery.

—THE TAOS NEWS

There are poems in this book that are etched in me now. Poems I'll return to again and again. Poems I'll teach. Poems I'll share with my own daughter. This book is a gift.

—MAGGIE SMITH

An exceptional collection of poems with pens in two worlds—Jewish and Sikh—and unafraid to mix faith with real life, with the body and sexuality, with loneliness, family, and grief. . . . These stunning poems go deep—to a soul level where they bring the reader in and share the holy here the world around us. You will be better for reading these poems, I know I am.

—KELLI RUSSELL AGODON

Brooke Sahni's poems exalt the borders between human and divine, child and woman, and her personal need to understand her inheritances. . . . In poems full of beauty and inquiry, Sahni takes nothing for granted.

—CONNIE VOISINE

In This Distance

In This Distance

Poems

Brooke Sahni

21st Century Poets, No. 39

TRP: The University Press of SHSU
Huntsville, Texas 77341

Library of Congress Cataloging-in-Publication Data
Names: Sahni, Brooke, author.
Title: In this distance : poems / Brooke Sahni.
Other titles: In this distance (Compilation)
Description: First edition. | Huntsville, Texas : TRP: The University Press of SHSU, [2025] | Notes on Desire, on Distance -- When Audre Lorde Says Erotic, I Hear Ecstatic -- An Ode to Esther Perel -- for the wild lavender -- Knowledge Deeply Born -- A Case Against Omitting the O in God -- An Ode to You, For You -- Esther Perel and Audre Lorde Go Dancing -- Kissing -- Esther Perel Talks to a Fifteen-Year-Old Girl -- Litany for Lorde & Lily -- In This Distance -- An Ode to the Minutes Before You Touch Me -- I Like to Imagine -- Adam -- Carve -- Politically Incorrect Ode -- Eve Leaves Eden -- Eve in the Red-light District -- Voyage -- The Fall -- Moon -- Perigee -- On Contemplating the Future of You, I Pull the Warrior Rune and it says, Divine -- Dear Eve -- Building -- Home -- Toward Eden -- Paradise -- Gravid -- Circulate -- On the Erotic -- On the Ecstatic -- Perhaps if we understood desire -- Trying to Write About God Again.
Identifiers: LCCN 2025006100 (print) | LCCN 2025006101 (ebook) | ISBN 9781680034301 (trade paperback) | ISBN 9781680034318 (ebook)
Subjects: LCSH: Desire--Poetry. | LCGFT: Poetry.
Classification: LCC PS3619.A3935 I54 2025 (print) | LCC PS3619.A3935 (ebook) | DDC 811/.6--dc23/eng/20250331
LC record available at https://lccn.loc.gov/2025006100
LC ebook record available at https://lccn.loc.gov/2025006101

FIRST EDITION

Cover art: *In This Distance* by Filippa Jean Edghill
Author photo by Alexandru Ovidiu Stoica

Cover design by Cody Gates, Happenstance Type-O-Rama
Interior design by Maureen Forys, Happenstance Type-O-Rama

Printed and bound in the United States of America
First Edition Copyright: 2025

TRP: The University Press of SHSU
Huntsville, Texas 77341
texasreviewpress.org

For J

Fire needs air; desire needs space and distance.

—ESTHER PEREL

The erotic is the nurturer or nursemaid
of all our deepest knowledge.

—AUDRE LORDE

Contents

Notes on Desire, on Distance

1.

When I'm crouched on my heels in front of the young dead buck, I can hear
the landscaper in the distance tell my mother that he thinks I'm beautiful.

2.

When my new lover asks me to spread my legs wider he says
Let me see how pretty you are, to bring himself closer to me.

3.

My mother, worried about death's scent
decides we need to move the body farther away from us, that distance is the remedy—

4.

There are too many reasons why he and I shouldn't be, so I'm hesitant
and therefore closed, only letting a small part of myself peek through to reach him.

5.

But there are no men around to help us with the unpleasant weight,
the landscaper gone, and so—

6.

I realize I'm not very good at having a casual relationship because I consider telling my man that I did it, that I moved the body all by myself, dragging it down into the woods, just so he'll think I'm brave.

7.

O, you, we say to one another from a distance. *O, you.* A proclamation of longing.

8.

When I get even closer, there is a wound so cavernous it appears infinite, an endless maw that stays open, almost as if the dead could *allow*, say, *yes*, to the flies and wasps who want so deeply to harmonize inside the flesh.

9.

Because we've been apart longer than we've been together, we word our desire out of distance. When we're ravenous, we say so. When we want it raw, we say so. When we want to devour each other's mouths, we say so. When we want the nighttime tenderness of soft limbs, we say so. *Cock. Spit. Night.* He says, *Kismet. O, you.* So much want, we are becoming made of words.

10.

My mother and I call Fish and Game and the kind female voice says that because the buck isn't near enough to any road, there's nothing they could do. *Leave it to the circle of life.* She said it two more times: *Leave it to the circle of life.* If her voice were flesh, it would be the tender side of a young girl's wrist.

11.

When he wanted me to spread, he pleaded, *O-pen.* I'm still not sure how I feel about the word *splay.* I still will not tell you of all the reasons he's forbidden, just that he said it two more times, *Open, open.*

12.

My mother ties a rope around the back legs and I watch as she drags the body over rocks, the head unapologetically thumping, and I wonder if the wound is getting wider. I wonder how much time it will take for the body to disintegrate. I wonder what animal might come tonight to eat the flesh. The phrase from my lover from a few days ago: *I want to eat you like a plains lion eats a gazelle out from the crotch first* or, *I suppose I'd like to eat you in some way—*

13.

as to taste you in mouth. It's not like my mother to move an animal body through the woods. As I watch her disappear farther, there are messages coming off of this distance: *My mother is brave,* and, *if my body were to lay out just like that in death I would be eaten away just the same.*

14.

When she returns she's crying about the body, talking of my grandparents who are bones beneath the ground. What is the point of all this living? As hospice nurse, my mother has tended to more dead bodies than most. *Something about the animal body,* she says. O, body. O, distance from the living to the dead.

15.

Tonight, with him at last, I remember how to say *Alive* without speaking. There is the word, again, cresting on his lips: *O-pen.* But I will not let him speak it. I will take his hands to my inner thighs and let him widen the sweet distance that keeps us, the living, always surrendering to the same chant: together we sing *Open,* together we plead *More.*

When Audre Lorde Says *Erotic*, I Hear *Ecstatic*

Because when she says *The erotic is knowledge deeply born* there is something so lovely in that phrasing,
I feel a moment of transcendence.

Because I'm called back to Sharon Olds's "After Making Love in Winter," where the body after
sex is blessed holy, rendered godly, full of light and even rebirth, so, in this way,

Lorde is right: the erotic is the opposite of pornography. Because the ecstatic is overwhelming
happiness *and* involves a mystic self-transcendence,

therefore, so much joy exists within just one small word, I agree
with Lorde when she says we should not separate the spiritual and the erotic—

because just the other day I read about a father who pulled glass out of his little girl's foot
not with his hands but with his mouth—

what about that sacred tenderness? And speaking of the mouth, what about what the mouth does
in order to get an olive down to its pit? What about the olive and its salty flesh?

Because I can perfectly recall the cadence of my grandfather's voice when calling my grandmother
Honey. Lorde, if the erotic is the personification of love, how could it not be full

of the ecstatic? No, we don't have to use *god*. Nor *man* nor *afterlife*. I think you said it best when
you said it's when your body stretches to music. When you're dancing. Writing a poem.

Making love. Examining an idea. Yes, I say *Ecstatic*. I might say *Holy*. I might word it *god*, then cross
it out and say *me* and *you*, because we are enough. Yes,

I believe the erotic is the ecstatic's twin, they are girls, of course, girls like the lilies
on the counter, with full bodies of their own

and mouths open to receive the sun, their scent almost as delicious and well-traveled
as lust because even this is not enough—

I rise to touch them.

An Ode to Esther Perel

I listen to the relationship therapist
talk about desire. There are so many beautiful ways
she words it: that love *is to have*, where desire *is to*
want. She says that we seek the Other in order to discover
some lost part of ourselves.

I love a poem that says maybe we fall in love
to see what we look like to someone else
and another that says love is allowing yourself
to say *yes* to a bee-sting in the heart. Scorpion-sting.

The man I desire is a Scorpio, more fire than water
and told me he wants to drink my mouth
like a kitten at her milk bowl.
Or did I say that to him?

O, Esther Perel, you spin
the erotic for a living, scholar, saint
of pleasure, the way you make *ravenous*, *want*,
and *distance* human, you with knowledge
deeply born, telling me things

I am certain I know somewhere
or used to know, how I think I love you
in a way I have loved myself
but have forgotten.

For the wild lavender

and the distance between us and the moon.
Us being us, we have to name it. Put small

words to a large thing. *Beautiful, silver, full.*
I love you

but will not tell you in
what ways, and this is what keeps
my desire full.

There are lines I could write, like *my love for you*
is a hidden swell, just for the pleasure

of imagining you crossing it out.
There is a wild lavender bush lit by the moon.

And when I muddle its purple between
my fingers, drawing it to my neck,

I remember you're sensitive to smell.
I apologize and you say,

It's not like I'm going to nuzzle you—so maybe
this is an elegy, for the scent on my skin

bittersweet reminder of all the ways you will not
touch me. No—

this is an ode. For the lavender and for
the moon, too, for the ecstatic distance

that keeps me begging, silently,
for you.

Knowledge Deeply Born

I read your essay first, then discovered I could listen, so I took my computer and a drink outside and sat with your voice and autumn that had just begun to bloom in the high desert. I mostly looked to the pines as I listened, but sometimes I glanced to the stilled image of your face, imagining the way your mouth would have moved speaking to a filled auditorium. I thought of the women, maybe shy women, scared women, hurt women, women wanting, all the women who needed your gospel the most, O Lorde,

my favorite part is when you say *Satisfaction doesn't have to be called god, marriage, man, afterlife*—I love
how much room that leaves, how much endless space for the most essential things to grow and yet remain unnamed, so in this way I do understand the comments on the screen, women writing *So, what is the erotic? Does anyone know what she's really talking about?* A mutual confusion spreading through cyberspace. And there are a lot of things I don't know, but I think I get this: something deeply rooted, and therefore, always, unnamable, unspeakable, I think of how my lover loves to call me a witch and I pretend to take offense—but really, I know he is trying to put a word to this thing brewing inside me, this thing I don't dare try to name.

A Case Against Omitting the O in God

I'll admit it: sometimes I do like it without the *o.*
Not out of respect, the reason some of my Jewish kin write it—g-d—
but because I like the way it looks. G-d.
So wholly unfinished, incomplete like the term itself,
so opposite of *ardent, fever,* or *cock, ache*
honeysuckle or even *moon* or *bloom,* with their double o's
so much like breasts. *God,*
so incapable of getting at what's most holy and reverent—
it doesn't even sound nice like *horoscope, willow, bewitch,*
catacomb, or *languid.*

But really, I love the *o,*
the letter, the sound, the shape.
How it makes me think of fullness,
the body's ecstasy cresting at the mouth
in the shape of an O. *O-pen, ode, orgasm, you.*
Because if we are going to assign a word
to all of the multiplicities,
it should at least have its center,
circular like the sun and moon and the earth,
circular and never-ending,

so when people see it on the page

they might be reminded of life—

and there is so much life.

Remember how good it felt to sup on the beloved?

Or to sit alone, needing no one, and autumn?

When autumn was bursting

all around you?

An Ode to *You*, For You

You, with three letters and an *o* in the center,
like god.

Like god,
there's worship.

Worship the distance
that keeps *you* in our lexicon,

us saying, *more of you, o, you.*

Or sometimes just you. *You* as a declaration,
you as longing, of course, as longing,

you as an elegy, all the parts of you
I don't know—to say no to you,

to say fuck you, how are you, keep you
maybe one day to be done with you,

to say *I don't need you*—

But first let us meet again
to sigh *yes*, to say *you*.
O, to say you.

Esther Perel & Audre Lorde Go Dancing

Audre wants a booth seat
but Esther is drawn
to the long, metal architecture
of the barstools. They compromise—
stand in a corner that's dark
but not hidden, where the neon
light can touch the tips
of their hair & they can watch
the bartender move her hips
while setting fire
to the open mouths of drinks.

The music is loud
& even though
they are standing
inches apart they feel like
they are yelling across
a great distance.
What have you been working on,
Audre shouts to Esther,
but Esther is pointing
to a couple across
the room. Audre
can only make out *limbs*
& *eye contact*—is frustrated,
they are both frustrated—
after all, how did they
end up here? In a bar
on a red-lit street?
An unknown
city where
everyone is dancing
with abandon & the music

is so loud they can't hear the brilliance
coming off of the other?
& even though it's all deafening,
they do like the feel
of something thumping
quietly in their hearts.

And you? Esther yells.
Audre is working on something
perfect, radical, complete,
Esther is sure, but her voice travels
& refracts. Esther is thrilled—
she could make out the part about
moving into sunlight against the body
of a woman, is convinced she
understands the context even though
Audre's voice floated into the music
& became something else.

Their voices
are hoarse, there is so much
to be heard from the other, but
they are tired of yelling,
tired of feeling percussion beat
their flesh and stand still
against it. So they take off
their jackets,
put their drinks down,
hand in hand,
they head toward the wild womb
of the party.
They close their eyes.
They are ready to write a new scripture.
They are ready to dance.

Kissing

It wasn't, for a long time, about sex, but the thrilling tide

of mouths. Kissing, what they asked us to do in school

if we dropped the siddur or anything with the word *god*.

We were kids, 7, 8, 9 years old, clumsy, so there was a lot

of kissing. Girl's mouths on the blue spine of the prayer book

which was said to hold the weight of god, so we were

kissing the entire universe. But the book didn't kiss back, neither did

the metal bar of my headboard that I loved to practice on, nor the men

and women who kissed in the movies, the kissing I found

so exciting and intangible. In front of adults

I always pretended to find kissing disgusting, too afraid

to admit to this wild thing inside me that ached, how all I wanted

was for one of the movie stars to reach through the glass

and show me what the tongue can do. First kiss,

girl in middle school who stabbed her tongue into my mouth.

When I pulled away, she pulled me back.

How could I forget the pre-kiss from the girl I loved—
my bully and my infatuation—how she laid
her long and beautiful body atop mine and put her entire face
into my neck giving me the gift of her breath, but not, ever,
giving me enough, so in this way my desire was always full.
And finally the boys. The boys who kissed badly,
the boys who kissed ok, and the few
who kissed so excellently, sex still felt beside the point.
Esther Perel says the kiss you imagine giving can be better
than the real thing—the sweet gift of the imagination,
how we can live in and make it anything we want—
and usually I would agree, but instead I feel as though
I have discovered kissing for the first time.
With you, baby, your mouth is an ocean
inviting me to swim.

Esther Perel Talks to a Fifteen-Year-Old Girl

The girl is fifteen, meaning she is alive like a newly budding
fruit tree and the world is both stunning and painful.
She's in her bedroom after a night out drinking on the streets

of her teendom, where she felt alive and insecure, and now
so lonely her bones hurt. She's already fallen in love deeply
and lost it, so she feels made of absence.

Across the room Esther sits atop a heap of clothes, wondering what she can say.
At first, her words come out in the same tone as her mother,
it will be ok, everything will be ok.

The girl turns to the wall, which makes Esther feel like a teenaged
girl, too. *Fine, be that way*, Esther says, noticing the way the girl,
all soft-limbed, wraps herself around the quilt,

remembering how fifteen-year-olds just want to love the world
and have it love them back. *This distance between you and him*
will grow something so large inside you—

The curl girls her body inward,
then it's just silence, the room filling heavy with their respective
longing. What can Esther say to reach her?

There was a boy, too, when I was fifteen, Esther says. She remembers
how he smelled in autumn. She describes his arms and when he
suddenly retreated away, how his distance

filled her. She moves backwards to childhood, a neighborhood
filled with Holocaust survivors, the contrast between
surviving and living, and the girl for the first time

moves—she doesn't face Esther, but moves her body closer to the wall,

leaving a space on the bed for Esther to fill. Esther walks over
and the two lay together, giving each other

permission to slowly drift away
and into each other.

Litany For Lorde & Lily

O, Lorde, even as a child praying to HaShem, I never believed in a god I could name,

I never believed in a king of the universe, I believed in the flesh, the trees,

the flesh of the girl, Lily, who held a power I couldn't name, Lily,

whose name was our incantation, at night at sleepovers we sat in circles, Lily, our chant

around the lunch table, Lily. Lorde,

we called her lord, and it was hard to love a thing that doesn't love you back—

but of course it made us want her more, Lorde

once she dragged her flip flop across the body of a lightning bug until the pavement

pulsed neon, just to show me how cruel and beautiful she could be, Lily, and I laughed

because to say otherwise was to disobey. Lorde,

if I had had your words as a girl, that satisfaction doesn't have to be called *god,*

maybe I would have given myself permission to see the ordinary for what it is—*holy,* to name

her breath sewn into my neck when she laid on top of me for what it was, *ecstatic,*

Lorde, maybe I would have sighed *Amen,* or maybe when she treated us unkindly, which

she always did, I would have found the strength to renounce, to say *Enough.* Lorde,

I wonder what it would look like if all the young, mean girls had your feminism,

I wonder what you might teach them and I wonder if I even want the Lilys of the world to be kind, enlightened, the young, mean girls who know how to harness power of out of beauty, who know the eroticism of restraint, who know how to give just a little to make the other want more, so singular and encompassing like god, so expert in their ability to charm and destroy, the young girls who leave us crawling, the young girls who teach us

how to pray.

In This Distance

Because I cannot have you

I tell you

how I want you. Together

we sanctify thirst raw

you

night cock ache tenderness inner

thigh stars swoon—

when?

Because we cannot feel one another, we write

a scripture born of longing

like the first people to have dreamt up Adam and Eve

writing a legacy of want, an apple that wasn't just an apple, but something

sweet and full and

deliciously

out of reach.

An Ode to the Minutes Before You Touch Me

For now, I am everything and you are everything.
The gift of the imagination is this:

I get to see myself how I want to be seen; I get to build myself
within the architecture of our desire.

We have not touched one another, or eaten together,
or danced, or laughed hard,

we haven't felt pain in the same vicinity or talked
about our childhoods. And still

I have been joyous under your gaze and words only,
you have lived a life inside this distance,

you say *Kismet,* even when our destiny
is one that hurts others.

But I am so near now I can practically taste you,
here blessing these moments before we touch,

because I know there is nothing sweeter than this—
the seconds before we step out

of one another's imagination
and into each other.

I Like to Imagine

It is our imagination that is responsible for love.

—ESTHER PEREL

I like to imagine Eve, naked, of course, falling in love with Adam. Not because he made her feel safe or comfortable, but because he made her feel ravenous. I like to imagine Eve imagining. Adam who had dissed her in the morning and gotten moody. Adam who said, *I'll be back soon* and wasn't. Now it's the golden hour and Eve, leaning against the tree, imagines a more prosperous tree and Adam with a woman with bigger tits, fuller lips, the two diving into each other's mouths—no one will ever kiss Eve the way he does—and Eve, feeling both desire and jealousy, the close cousins of want, gets wet. The more she imagines, the wetter she gets. Adam finding beauty without her, Adam at a distance eating thinly sliced figs from the navel of another, Adam so capable of forgetting her for an afternoon and so Eve never wanted him more. And because she aches, she reaches. The fruit is sweet. On her second bite he sneaks up behind her, grabbing her at the ribs. *I missed you,* he says. So she tosses the fruit into the brush and takes his hand in to feel her.

Adam

Because he's a Scorpio, he's brought with him some strange, alluring gift. A bone, a feather, something slight and ephemeral—a gentle reminder that he could be gone, too. If Adam were a Scorpio, then maybe he would have been born in late October, my favorite season, the dark season—fall. At night, with Eve, he would have talked abstractly about the world because back then everything was magic—the lack of language, luminous, lack of science to name even the sunset or the smell of fruit ripening on the tree. I like to imagine how beautiful it all would have been. And terrifying, like the Scorpio, all night and darkness, mystery and abandon. Unabashed about nakedness, first kiss without a word for *swoon*—all feeling and flesh. Back when everything was so close without having the word *perigee.* And the moon was so close. Eve, sticking out her tongue, could almost taste it, and Adam knew she was beautiful. He felt more beautiful in her presence. And he forgot about god, though god was so close, and believed he had created the world. He whispered to Eve imperfect explanations: *this is how,* and *this is why.*

Carve

In the story, Eve came from Adam. The message: a woman cannot exist without a man.
I cannot help my subconscious. In my dream, I am clay and you carve my pussy with your tongue.
You carve and I do not crave. There is no craving yet, you are merely performing
an essential task. My beloved, in the dream you are drawing in my folds
and canyons with your mouth. You are working your tongue until I am done.
I do not resist. I do not tell you I don't need you to divine me,
I do not tell you how I was born knowing my femaleness, how I know every
crease and fold. That when I share that part of myself with you, I never mistake it
to be yours. In the dream, I look down at your mouth there,
my brown, earthen self becoming animated. Normally I would call out.
But here, in this latent passage, I surrender. You have important work to do.

Politically Incorrect Ode

Just for today, I'd like to forget about feminism.
I'd like to forget about Lorde and bow
to a new wave of thought.
I'm talking about you.
I'd like to forget that women do not belong
to men, or to anyone.
I'd like to forget about these poems—
the endless search for my autonomy
and the deep knowledge that I am most truly myself
within myself.
Today I want to dissolve
into the creases of your words; I want to escape
into the Edens of your flesh.
I do not want to eat
but be eaten.
Today I am the sacrament, not the altar.
Today I will wear your favorite scent because
you love it, and when you tell me
I'm beautiful, it will be you I am beautiful for. I will open
my legs as wide as I can— today, I would break
in two for you.
I do not want to hear myself
say my own name—not once.
Today I want to be no one else's
but yours.

Eve Leaves Eden

Because she hasn't been alone since she was born. Because the romance has worn off. Because she has been here for eternity, and yes, things can be too perfect. Here, it is always summer and the fruit trees are always in bloom. Adam has shown a new devotion to her, which makes her want him less. The serpent has started to tell her stories of places with hardened edges, buildings, and balconies, and people with tormented expressions. He tells her tales in whispers over firelight while Adam is cooking dinner. There are places with traffic and men with lean and muscular bodies. In her imagination, Eve begins walking, and as she walks, she comes into herself. There is a man in the city who is waiting for her, his body adorned in tattoos with a tender voice and hands that pin her down to a soft bed. There are women, too, the serpent says. Their cheeks shine red, and they will tease you, too. In the city, there are fruit markets, but more grease, so many things to make a body feel good in the moment, you might, the snake warns, feel really bad later. But Eve, holding onto the snake's every word, wants to feel some anguish while being pinned down to a bed by a man with strong hands. She begins her voyage, away from her home, and it is the last thing the snake said that pulls her forward: *in this new world, there are people who call out to god not because they believe, but simply because they feel good. They sing, oh, god, oh, oh.*

Eve in the Red-light District

She arrives and it is all terrifying.

She cannot believe she has lived this long without

being terrified of love.

Voyage

In desire we need a bridge to cross.

—ESTHER PEREL

I was given a taste and I wanted more.
It's only when I am writing that I think
to metaphor you *forbidden fruit,*
though sometimes I do forget that you do not
belong to me, nor I
to you.

*

I am thinking about what it means to belong
to someone,
how desire
needs space and air,
how when we are apart, I long to voyage,
how when we are together,
we tether.

*

I live in an Eden now, on 4 acres.
If asked a year ago what I wanted,
it would have been this: land, trees,
a place of my own. To set roots.
And now—

*

The first week we spend together,
you teach your students from home. Each morning
I awake in your bed listening to you spin
words about the circulatory system.

*

Circulation means *the continuous motion*
by which the blood travels
through all parts of the body
under the action of the heart.

*

With every man I have loved,
we have felt one another's pulse, as though
the action is an inevitability of intimacy,
a simple way to say, *I feel you.*
*
I read about the blood as exile
and as punishment and feel guilty
that I can write an entire poem
about the blood as love.

The heart as an organ that is movement.

*

Lorde moving into sunlight.

*

Us moving closer through language until

you move into me.

*

I do not believe in a god that wants us
to feel guilty.

I packed my things and that was ritual,
I left my home, and that was sacrament.
Though I was leaving, it felt like a return.

*

We had a taste and wanted more.
        We were apart for two months, writing
you in so many ways,
        a voyage of language,
an unfulfilled beginning.

We wrote out *ache* in so many ways,
I came closer to you.

*

The relationship therapist says
affairs are about discovering a lost part
of ourselves—

I am finding that eroticism is about creative
power.
    That when I write about you, I am
bridging a distance between myself
      and myself.

*

After a week of the circulatory system, you
give your students a test. By then we are apart

    again, and you send me a message: *best question*
on the test: why do you think the heart is
      associated with the notion of love?

    You record yourself reading your favorite answers:
        When you are in love, your heart beats faster so you know
            you are alive.

*

What would I tell a future self about you?
That Eden seemed like a place to go to, not
a place that was already mine.

*

I am writing a book that is a prayer:
That we may circulate each other.
That our love may be full
but never fulfilled.

*

What I would give to hear you say, again
tricuspid, to feel a rush of blood.

In this distance, I tell you

how I worry

that soon I will confuse the red-light district
for paradise.

I will travel home

not knowing which direction is to

or away

from you.

The Fall

We were together   far from any green

snow came

              down

                                and the world was gray
but I couldn't help but think

Crimson
              violet
                                nectar
                                                you.

And I knew

my first bite would hold a bitterness
and I knew   you were sweeter for it

so I took
and the snow came

              down harder

and everything inside skipped spring and burst

              into summer.

Moon

And then everything was full.
And still we wanted more.

So we turned on a star projector, so even our skin had stars, and
we, godlike, chose the color of the nebula—

we chose red. I wonder if I should say, *shame on us*
for not allowing the real thing to satiate—

the moon was full and there were stars.
To compensate for distance

I didn't leave your apartment for a week.
We drank juice, ate eggs.

I have always been drawn to the moon like a feminine birthright.
Without trying, I have loved it.

The moon was full and we wanted more. We ate bread.
Sometimes when I am full I think I love the world as much

as I possibly could. Sometimes I think I love the word as much as the real thing,
the sound and shape of *moon* on the page, full.

Sometimes when I write it I feel satiated.
It snowed and snowed and you said something beautiful

about our days being weighed down by the world and its white devour.
Soon *absence* became abstract, everything was heavy and filled.

And when we no longer had a want for words,
we carved thick passages with our tongues,

we breathed each other and were full.
And although we didn't need to, at night we took turns whispering, *moon*

as softly as we possibly could, and still.
Because it was your mouth to my ear, the word couldn't bare lightness,

it sunk into me, craterless.
I could practically taste its silver going down.

Perigee

In the beginning I was so full on you I could hardly eat.
New lovers, you fed me each piece of your novelty—

arms, breath, skin, words—

in bed together for days, we barely moved.
Yes, there was sun to feed us.

Now I am thinking it's absence that we need
in order to know we're full.

In the beginning I could watch you across a room
and delight in what existed in between

our distance. Because I didn't know you,
I believed, again, we were creating something new.

Everything was novel and nothing was full,
so we were filled.

My beloved, I love you, but you are so close now.

Just for a moment I'd like to touch you in the dark
and not mistake you as mine.

On Contemplating the Future of You, I Pull the Warrior Rune and it Says *Divine*.

*

I wonder what will come of this—who I will be in the wake of our fall. The rune says *Divine.* Says,
When this rune comes in response to a relationship issue, it indicates that the relationship is timely and providential.

*

Audre says the erotic is the divine within ourselves and I believe her.

*

Esther says an affair is an attempt to recover some lost part of ourselves and I believe her, too.

*

I am collecting knowledge, and sometimes it weighs me down
and other times the words of others lift me.

*

What will you show me about myself that I have forgotten?
Who will you become in the wake of my absence?
What part of myself can I not see?
What part of the tree do you want to take?

*

Holy is the way we look at one another in order to see ourselves anew.
Something ecstatic blooms.

*

I do not know what will come of this, or if the rune is right—
But we've already fallen, so let there be paradise.
We've already taken the fruit, so let there be knowledge.
And I have prayed and felt like god.

*

Audre and Esther say the erotic, like god, lives within our bodies
and baby, tonight I feel god swirling all around us—

*

remember how you took your fingers to your mouth
just to lick me off of you? And how when I made you come,
it was me I was coming into?

Dear Eve,

Maybe paradise is a place we long to enter; maybe we eat the apple simply
to remember what is sweet.
I have been away from home and thinking of you. Sometimes I want to call you *Eden*—
just the idea of you bridges a distance between my pleasure and my sin.
Where did you discover pleasure doesn't mean *god* or *man*
or *Adam*? Did the ecstatic come to you as a golden light inside the chest? Afterall,
we were given flesh, so let us embrace the ecstatic difference between my body
and yours. For example, when I touch him, I think of your pleasure and your sin.
In the Book, god classified Eden as wet.
In my beloved's bed he calls on my wetness as if it's promised.
He calls me to my knees and when I am full on him, Eve, it is you
I thank for knowing how to revel in the sin
of his sweetness.

Building

Because you feel so good
I can't help but think of destruction.
At home, my partner is building our house,
here, I reinvent under your touch.

I thought that pleasure was something owed to me,
that to be human was to take of the fruit.
At home, spring is blooming and my beloved is building
and he sends me pictures of tall grasses, our river.

I have lived so long in the low desert,
I've forgotten what to do with green.
Here, we are entwined like a vine grown out of an endless Eden.
I take of your flesh and you take of mine.

I could worship or I could confess and often I do both.
Recently everything has been built around you,
but home is still a place I long for,
our desire a thing that exists inside

what's fallen. Because even under the pleasure of you,
something is different now.
When I take a bite, I pray it is the last.
I hope to god to grow full on you.

Home

Humans are destroying the natural world, but the birds are singing
in a tune that feels like a prayer.
The neighbors who live across from us descend
their mountain to visit, and we offer them tea and wine.
They ask us if we've seen the angels, say the woman who lived
on our land before us said she saw angels.
Before you can answer, I say, *no, no we haven't seen them.*
But I haven't been here long, always coming and going, always returning
to the ways in which you've made this place more beautiful. And who am I to believe
this land couldn't stand to hold the presence of the divine, when I've known
my whole life about the trees and what happens to them at dusk?
I take your hand. A hummingbird whirs by
and later, after everyone is gone and we are close,
I tell you, *I want to stay. I want to see them, too.*

Toward Eden

Eve reached and was punished.

And sometimes I think I am given too much.

Sometimes I want to destroy my own making.

I don't believe in the Fall.

I believe in desire as an Eden we long to enter.

That even when we are full, we ache for more.

We clear the land of trees only to plant more,

to have a home in beauty and still long to leave.

But this isn't about self-destruction.

It's about a world where beauty keeps coming for us.

It's about the soft power of human muscle,

your arm, then, exquisitely designed to reach,

and for my body's ability

to soften at its approach.

Paradise

She dreamt of her days lived, they were that sweet. In the morning there were omelets stuffed with goat cheese, and in the afternoon, espresso in the park, the one with the pond and long-necked swans that coasted along the water's glass skin; there were movie theaters and bars and just when Eve thought there was enough, there were buses and trains to remind her there was more. Each night, a different man. She called one of them *Nectarine*, and the other *Passion Fruit*—they all tasted delicious. When they took of her mouth, they bowed before drinking, and she grew more joyous with each slurp. And at night, after they were gone, she dreamt of tomorrow: a croissant for breakfast, a concert and French fries at lunchtime, and at night, her favorite man would visit. Though she resisted the idea, she couldn't help it—she called this one *Apple*. With him she didn't think about god. Not once.

Gravid

But then, she was really full. Apple wasn't forbidden or elusive, but loving, stable, even a little needy. Last night, with Apple's head resting on her stomach, Eve told him about Adam and Apple listened, said that Adam sounded like a good man but that he could love her until the end of the world, that he'd loved her since the beginning of time. For a moment, Eve felt a rush of blood. She felt his cock ache, she let him into her. In the morning, she found herself ravenous. She got herself a bloody steak and she ate and ate and felt an ache.

Circulate

1.
She returned.
The animals lifted their heavy heads
to gaze upon her.
Adam stood.
His face said, *I missed you,* said,
I'm older now, said,
Come closer.

2.

In this distance, I tell you
that I made it safely, that for a year now, you have been my sanctuary—
first your words, then the ecstatic Eden
of your flesh. We are far again.
Honestly, I could keep wording you into me, I could voyage
and return.
Instead, I say *I'm home now. There is a house*
in the woods that's mine—
I enter.

3.

Eve, Adam says, *I discovered this while you were gone.* He holds it up, it's the color of blush. *I call it Longing Fruit. And this,* he says, placing his fingers around the soft bulge at the center of his neck, *it's like a small apple inside my throat.* Suddenly, Eve remembers want. And then Adam asks *Eve, was it paradise there?* And Eve, looking at his gorgeous neck, doesn't know the answer or where paradise is, so she inches closer, turns her head to the side and takes a bite.

4.

I've returned and our land is in heat.
Everything is green again and the river reminds me
that arriving is all relative.
I've driven hundreds of miles across the desert to return to you,
Eden is still taking on new meaning.
You're up on the hill planting apple trees and I
don't think about metaphor or these poems.
I still don't believe in the Fall, but I'm sorry.
I see you in the light.
That first apple is yours.

5.

All spring we've watched the hummingbirds zip and return, zip
        and return, zip and return to their red feeders. There is so much beauty
here and it's all within reach. Leaning against you, I confess that sometimes
        I take it for granted, as if this pleasure were owed to me,
and when I'm not taking it for granted, I feel the weight of the world against me,
        that impenetrable guilt for how humans are ruining the environment.
What can we do? I ask you, who has always been more in touch with the natural world.
        And you open your arms like Moses and say
We start here, we will be good to what's in front of us.

6.

The hummingbirds are drinking so much nectar, we buy another feeder. Instead of three plastic flowers, this new one has a full circle of eight. If I were to call this summer anything, it might be, Summer of Trying to Forget You, or Summer of Trying to See Beauty in What's Close. Or maybe just Summer of the Hummingbirds, how they zip and return, zip and return, zip away and return to a point of sweetness—this nectar that we make for them over and over and offer it gladly because we know, without fail, they will return to take it.

7.

I've seen you in every season except this one, I tell you. Fall, winter, spring. It's so hot when we speak, my blood pumps to all the parts I don't want it to: my pussy, of course, and even my neck, ghost of the spot where you've touched me gently. And then, god dammit I feel my heart. Always the heart.

Are you full on me? you ask again. And I think if I reply in a rhythm that beats, you might

believe me: *I'm trying, I'm trying.*

8.

I am alone. I am outside and god is so close
by which I mean I am feeling alive in my body.
The world is still here. There is the sky and the trees.
Dusk is near, cooling things, but my skin
is still warm from the day and my blood pumps
just for me.

On the Erotic

I do not need the word/to know/what is holy/inside of me/to know
how to worship/to know to worship is to/recognize/that ineffable sweetness/when you call/
me/sweetness/to know the fruits of my hunger/to know intuitively how to praise/your body/
to know to love/your body/is holy/to love anything at all/the wind/by way of summertime/
curtains/to hear a whisper and think it/is you/to be blessed to realize/it is me/to know the
apple is mine/to know, again,/how to give it to you

Today I am yours.
Just for today give me this.
It's summer again.

On the Ecstatic

/give me you/until I am given myself back again/over and over we are given this/ internal house/o, joy.

Sunlight across skin,
wind through cotton curtains, O.
I will name it later.

Perhaps if we understood desire,

After Kelli Russell Agodon

we would no longer desire. No longer need the word, have no need for *raw* or *ravenous, tenderness* or O or *you.* We would be satiated on love and stability and no longer seek the red-light district of the mind and body. If we understood desire we would not desire. Not food, because it would be ordinary; brie and olives and wine would be rendered mundane like white bread; the body, the breasts, the swell of a cock—there wouldn't be *swell* or *cock,* everything would be anatomical, all penis and vagina, *pussy* would be obsolete; flesh would become *flab, tit* would become *spout*—musical masterpieces, mere tunes, David, mere rock, your body and my body would no longer be granted the thrill of a lustrous beginning or a devastating but beautiful end, but the perpetual middle of a long and lonely book.

Trying to Write About God Again

It's summer, season of maturity,

bloom embodied, neither retreating nor in progress.

I'm talking about fullness.

I took a walk and embraced the season's gravity.

Opulence and fruit.

At home now, I write the word *god* on the page.

I think of you, my beloved, how one day you will be gone

and god, again, will bloom in absence.

You are far and I pray

not to god who is far, but to distance

that keeps me tethered.

I know it is fruitless to try.

Maybe not because it is hard, but because it is too easy,

"god" too numerous

I could write it out of anything.

The fig I plucked in secret on my walk,

its warmth and ineffable sweetness—

I could write anything about the flesh or the trees,

the time I first heard you recite a poem from memory,

what lifted from me and returned.

Without thinking, I write it over and over: *god, god, god,*

just to let the mind go blank,

just to hear the word render itself meaningless,

just for the pleasure of circular movement,

just for pleasure.

Acknowledgments

"Adam," *Alaska Quarterly*

"Toward Eden," *Anthropocene*

"Kissing," "Esther Perel & Audre Lorde Go Dancing," *Beaver Magazine*

"An Ode to *You*, For You," "A Case Against Omitting the O in God," *Boulevard*

"Paradise," *The Cincinnati Review*

"I Like to Imagine," "Perigee," *Diode*

"Eve Leaves Eden," *EcoTheo Review*

"Eve Leaves Eden," *Between Paradise & Earth: Eve Poems*

"Notes on Desire, on Distance," *Frontier Poetry*

"For the wild lavender," *Glass: A Journal of Poetry*

"Litany for Lorde & Lily," "Carve," "Trying to Write About God Again," "The Fall, *The Laurel Review, Breaking the Glass: A Contemporary Jewish Poetry Anthology*

"An Ode to Esther Perel," *Poet Lore*

"When Audre Lorde Says *Erotic*, I Hear *Ecstatic*," *Sixth Finch*

"Perhaps if we understood desire," *South Dakota Review*

"Paradise," *Verse Daily*

"Eve Leaves Eden," *Verse Daily*

"Moon," *Zocalo Public Square*

I'd like to thank Luke Hankins and Tyler Truman Julian for reading these poems and offering their time and insight. Thanks to TRP, especially J. Bruce Fuller and Charlie Tobin for supporting my poetry and giving two of my books a home.

Thank you to Audre Lorde and Esther Perel whose ideas on the erotic moved through me and moved me. It was a joy to be in conversation with their work.

About the Author

Brooke Sahni is the author of *Before I Had the Word* (TRP, 2021), which won The X. J. Kennedy Poetry Prize. She is also the author of *Divining* (Orison Books, 2020), which won the Orison Chapbook Prize. Her poetry and fiction have appeared in journals such as *Alaska Quarterly, Missouri Review, The Cincinnati Review, Verse Daily, 32 Poems, Prairie Schooner, Nimrod, Indiana Review,* and elsewhere. She lives in the high desert mountains of Arizona.

21st Century Poets

21st Century Poets is a collection of full-length poetry books by TRP authors whose first book of poetry was released after the year 2000.

Books in this series

No. 001 — Kendall Dunkelberg—*Time Capsules*

No. 002 — William Bedford Clark—*Blue Norther and Other Poems*

No. 003 — Karla K. Morton—*Names We've Never Known*

No. 004 — Ben Greer—*The Bright House*

No. 005 — Beryl Lawn—*Poems from Both Sides of the Fence*

No. 006 — Swep Lovitt—*Sometimes the World Is Too Beautiful*

No. 007 — William Wright—*Bledsoe*

No. 008 — Sarah Cortez—*Walking Home*

No. 009 — Jesse Graves—*Tennessee Landscape with Blighted Pine*

No. 010 — Richard Boada—*The Error of Nostalgia*

No. 011 — Sarah Cortez—*Cold Blue Steel*

No. 012 — David Havird—*Map Home*

No. 013 — Beryl Lawn—*More Poems from Both Sides of the Fence*

No. 014 — Jesse Graves—*Basin Ghosts*

No. 015 — Karla K. Morton—*A Constant State of Leaping*

No. 016 — Kendall Dunkelberg—*Barrier Island Suite*

No. 017 — Stephen Gibson—*The Garden of Earthly Delights*

No. 018 — Karla K. Morton—*Accidental Origami: New and Selected Works*

No. 019 — Karla K. Morton—*Wooden Lions*

No. 020 — Mary Morris—Enter *Water, Swimmer*

No. 021 — Elisabeth Murawski—*Heiress*

No. 022 — Randall Watson—*The Geometry of Wishes*

No. 023 — Sarah Kain Gutowski—*Fabulous Beast*

No. 024 — Jennifer Sperry Steinorth—*A Wake with Nine Shades*

No. 025 — Mary Morris—*Dear October*

No. 026 — Andrew Hemmert—*Sawgrass Sky*

No. 027 — Matt W. Miller—*Tender the River*

No. 028 — Jesse Graves—*Tennessee Landscape with Blighted Pine* (10th Anniversary Edition)

No. 029 — Forrest Rapier—*As the Den Burns*

No. 030 — Sarah Audsley—*Landlock X*

No. 031 — Luke Johnson—*Quiver*

No. 032 — Sarah Kain Gutowski—*The Familiar*

No. 033 — Joshua Robbins—*Eschatology in Crayon Wax*

No. 034 — Theodora Ziolkowski—*Ghostlit*

No. 035 — Kimberly Ann Priest—*tether & lung*

No. 036 — Mary Morris—*Lanterns in the Night Market*

No. 037 — Daniel Lassell—*Frame Inside a Frame*

No. 038 — Luke Johnson—*Distributary*

No. 039 — Brooke Sahni—*In This Distance*

No. 040 — Randall James Tyrone—*City of Dis*

No. 041 — Ryan Vine—*The Cave*